# WORKBOOK

A 99 page printable workbook you can use today!

BY LESLIE KOENIG, MD

STRESSRELIEFSURIVALGUIDE.COM

# A NOTE FROM THE AUTHOR

WELCOME, MY BEAUTIFUL FRIEND.

After 12 years of being an emergency medicine doctor, I've seen a thing or two about stress. When I was deployed to Afghanistan I saw it there also, in the most extreme environments with the highest trained warriors in history. I had to learn a *lot* of quick ways to guide patients through their worst experiences, through the fear to a place of stability.

This is a **no frills, right to the point checklist** of things to do when you feel powerless. There is **no prior experience necessary.** It's not a treatment plan, it is not a substitute for medical care. This is a list of things I have found that really, really work.

Despite all the information out there, extreme stress still comes in to the emergency room. At its most extreme, you can feel powerless, afraid, and misunderstood. Sometimes it's hard to recognize because you feel your body is wrong and your mind is fine. Even if you do have a real medical problem, it's hard to not be anxious about it!

Congratulations on recognizing that you have stress, and also that you are seeking ways to make it better. It is my hope this workbook is a backup for when the anxiety hits in a BIG WAY.

There are fantastic <u>daily practices</u> which **I highly recommend**, such as meditation and exercise. Medication is also extremely healing for countless people. Be sure you sleep and eat right. The tips here are tools *in addition* to these therapies, for when you feel on the verge of an attack, or even in the throes of an attack. Of course if you feel like you are having an emergency, go to the ER or call 911. These tips will help you on the way.

This is a quick guide to expand on the STRESS RELIEF QUICK CARD and follow along with the STRESS RELIEF SURVIVAL GUIDE VIDEO COURSE so you feel empowered and can face extreme stress with minimal preparation. You can do this. You are not alone. Let your light shine.

*Leslie Koenig, MD*

Leslie Koenig, MD
www.StressReliefSurvivalGuide.com

# STRESS SURVIVAL CHECKLIST
## CALMING TIPS THAT ARE QUICK AND TO THE POINT

**INSTRUCTIONS**: Each technique stands on its own, and may have varying results based on your situation. The more technical tips are at the top, and the most basic are at the bottom. Sort of a reverse "escalation of force." Work your way down, and once done, fill out the recovery worksheets with any insight you gained.

- [ ] RAIN / OODA LOOP- BONUS!!
- [ ] TAPPING
- [ ] 54321 OR 333 RULE
- [ ] BATTERY TECHNIQUE
- [ ] MIRROR MEDITATION
- [ ] HOT SHOWER VS ICE MAN
- [ ] THUMB SQUEEZE TECHNIQUE
- [ ] IN THE HERE, IN THE NOW
- [ ] PACED BREATHING
- [ ] SHOCK THE SENSES
- [ ] REBREATHING

STRESSRELIEFSURVIVALGUIDE.COM | © 2020 LESLIE KOENIG, MD

# WHERE DO I START?
## START WITH THE FIRST STEP

WHAT'S YOUR ZONE?
Start with the top exercise and work down

## YELLOW: ELEVATED

- <u>FATIGUED, EXHAUSTED</u>

    RAIN / OODA LOOP

    TAPPING

    54321 OR 333 RULE

    BATTERY TECHNIQUE

## ORANGE: HIGH

- <u>ANGER, ANXIETY</u>

    MIRROR MEDITATION

    HOT SHOWER VS ICE MAN

    THUMB SQUEEZE TECHNIQUE

    IN THE HERE, IN THE NOW

## RED: CRITICAL

- <u>BURNED OUT, BREAKING DOWN</u>

    PACED BREATHING

    SHOCK THE SENSES

    REBREATHING

STRESSRELIEFSURVIVALGUIDE.COM | © 2020 LESLIE KOENIG, MD

# IT'S OK TO NOT BE OK
## BREAK DOWN THE FIRST STEP

I DON'T KNOW IF I CAN DO THIS.. *(HINT: <u>YOU CAN</u>)*
Maybe deciding what zone you're in can be tough. What thoughts do you recognize?

## YELLOW: ELEVATED

- <u>FATIGUED, EXHAUSTED</u>

"I JUST NEED A BREAK"

"TOMORROW WILL BE EASIER?"

"I JUST NEED SOME HELP"

"THIS ISN'T GOOD FOR ME"

## ORANGE: HIGH

- <u>ANGER, ANXIETY</u>

"EVERYTHING IS AGAINST ME"

"THINGS WILL NEVER CHANGE"

"MY WORLD IS CRASHING IN"

"NOTHING IS ENOUGH"

## RED: CRITICAL

- <u>BURNED OUT, BREAKING DOWN</u>

"I CAN'T TAKE THIS ANYMORE"

"I'M LOSING MY MIND, I'M DONE"

"IT'S TOO MUCH, I QUIT"

"I FEEL LIKE I'M DYING"

STRESSRELIEFSURVIVALGUIDE.COM | © 2020 LESLIE KOENIG, MD

# DON'T FORGET

### SIMPLE SOLUTIONS

## IT'S THE LITTLE THINGS

When stress comes into the ER, we start with many simple, easy steps. Under stress at home though, this list can be impossible to remember. They seem very basic and intuitive, so don't forget to start small. **Small changes over time lead to massive results.**

- [ ] LAY DOWN
- [ ] LIGHTS OFF
- [ ] DRINK WATER OR TEA
- [ ] PHONE IN ANOTHER ROOM
- [ ] <u>CALL</u> A FRIEND
- [ ] LISTEN TO MUSIC
- [ ] WALK AWAY
- [ ] GO OUTSIDE
- [ ] COUNT YOUR BLESSINGS
- [ ] DO SOMETHING NICE FOR SOMEONE
- [ ] EXERCISE
- [ ] WATCH A COMEDY

# BONUS! RAIN OODA
## *workbook*

STRESSRELIEFSURVIVALGUIDE.COM | © 2020 LESLIE KOENIG, MD

# RAIN TECHNIQUE
## BONUS- FOR INTROSPECTION

## What is RAIN?

RAIN is an acronym for mindfulness and compassion:

> **R: Recognize** a strong emotion
>
> **A: Accept** that it is there
>
> **I: Investigate** inwards
>
> **N: Nurture** yourself in a nice way

How do I do RAIN?

**Recognize** you're experiencing anxiety. Is masked by fear? Anger? Self doubt? Maybe your attention got triggered by noticing a fast heart rate or a clenched stomach. This is the first step- just *knowing*.

**Accept** and allow what is happening to just *Be*. No judgment, no labels, no Why. Say to yourself "oh hey, hello" or "well look at that. There it is." Think of it like a passing cloud.

**Investigate** what led up to this point. Now that you're in a neutral mindset, look at reasons *Why* and *Where*. Are you overburdened? Did you get enough sleep? Did you skip your gratitude meditation? *Where* do you notice this, in your chest or your stomach? Feel where it is, literally.

**Nurture** yourself the way your higher power might speak to you. What might a good friend say? What would the best version of yourself tell you right now? Some phrases might be "you can do this. I am love. I am strong, you have strength. I am able." Find something that resonates and sounds right. Start soft and get louder an louder. You can do this.

# RAIN: WORKSHEET 1

AFTER THE RAIN

**What made you Recognize?**

**Were you able to Accept?  What did/didn't help?**

**What in the Investigation was most helpful?  Did you gain any clarity?**

**What phrases in Nurturing struck a chord?  What felt Right?**

# RAIN WORKSHEET 2
### AFTER THE RAIN

HOW LONG DID IT TAKE:

- 5 minutes
- 15 minutes
- 45 minutes

HOW OFTEN WILL I DO IT:

- Daily
- Weekly
- Monthly

HOW I WANT TO FEEL:

- Joyful
- Grateful
- Balanced
- Relaxed
- Loved
- Happy
- Other:

DID MAKING THE TIME HELP?

HOW WILL I REMIND MYSELF?

HOW WILL I KNOW IT'S WORKING?

# RAIN WORKSHEET 3

### AFTER THE RAIN

**INSTRUCTIONS**: Rest in the awareness you now have. Reflect back on the process and notice your internal before/after. Write the thoughts down here.

NEGATIVE THOUGHT:					POSITIVE AFFIRMATION:

NEGATIVE THOUGHT:					POSITIVE AFFIRMATION:

NEGATIVE THOUGHT:					POSITIVE AFFIRMATION:

NEGATIVE THOUGHT:					POSITIVE AFFIRMATION:

# RAIN WORKSHEET 4

#### AFTER THE RAIN

**QUESTION #1:** What are your goals and vision for the future?

**QUESTION #2:** What obstacles are in the way of your goals and vision?

**QUESTION #3:** What more could you do to reach your goals and vision?

# OODA LOOP
## BONUS- FOR THE MILITARY MINDSET

## What is the OODA Loop?

OODA Loop is a strategy to rapidly WIN- I applied it to stress.

> **O: Observe** a strong emotion
>
> **O: Orient** to what is there
>
> **D: Decide** what caused the emotion or its effects
>
> **A: Act** talk to yourself in a nice way

How do I do the OODA Loop for myself?

**Observe** you're feeling some threat. Is masked by fear? Anger? Self doubt? Maybe your attention got triggered by noticing a fast heart rate or a clenched stomach. This is the first step- just *knowing*. This is **situational awareness**.

**Orient** and allow what is happening to just *Be*. No judgment, no labels, no Why. Say to yourself "oh hey, hello" or "well look at that. There it is." Think of it like a passing cloud. As Jocko says "Detach for clear thinking. Mentally step back."

**Decide** what led up to this point. Investigate inwards. Now that you're in a neutral mindset, look at reasons *Why* and *Where*. Are you overburdened? Did you get enough sleep? Did you skip your workout? *Where* do you notice this, in your chest or your stomach? Feel where it is, literally.

**Act.** This is done in the mind- where the battle started. Talk to yourself the way your higher power might speak to you. What might a good friend or mentor say? What would the best version of yourself tell you right now? Some phrases might be "You can do this. I am love. I am strong. You have strength. I am able." Find something that resonates and sounds right. Cuss words are totally fine if it makes you smile. Start soft and get louder an louder. You can Fing do this.

# OODA: WORKSHEET 1

### AFTER ACTION REPORT

**What made you Observe or get ahold of situational awareness?**

**Were you able to Orient? What did/didn't help?**

**What in the Decision was most helpful? Did you gain any clarity?**

**What phrases in Act struck a chord? What felt Right?**

# OODA WORKSHEET 2
### AFTER ACTION REPORT

HOW LONG DID IT TAKE:

- 5 minutes
- 15 minutes
- 45 minutes

HOW OFTEN WILL I DO IT:

- Daily
- Weekly
- Monthly

HOW I WANT TO FEEL:

- Joyful
- Grateful
- Balanced
- Relaxed
- Loved
- Happy
- Other:

DID MAKING THE TIME HELP?

HOW WILL I REMIND MYSELF?

HOW WILL I KNOW IT'S WORKING?

STRESSRELIEFSURVIVALGUIDE.COM | © 2020 LESLIE KOENIG, MD

# OODA WORKSHEET 3
### AFTER ACTION REPORT

**INSTRUCTIONS**: Rest in the awareness you now have. Reflect back on the process and notice your internal before/after. Write the thoughts down here.

NEGATIVE THOUGHT:                POSITIVE AFFIRMATION:

NEGATIVE THOUGHT:                POSITIVE AFFIRMATION:

NEGATIVE THOUGHT:                POSITIVE AFFIRMATION:

NEGATIVE THOUGHT:                POSITIVE AFFIRMATION:

STRESSRELIEFSURVIVALGUIDE.COM | © 2020 LESLIE KOENIG, MD

# OODA WORKSHEET 4
## AFTER ACTION REPORT

**QUESTION #1:** What are your goals and vision for the future?

**QUESTION #2:** What obstacles are in the way of your goals and vision?

**QUESTION #3:** What more could you do to reach your goals and vision?

# RAIN/OODA RESOURCES
NOTES AND FURTHER RESOURCES

- Book : **"Radical Compassion: Learning to Love Yourself and Your World with the Practice of RAIN" -** by Tara Brach

- Podcast: **"Ten Percent Happier with Dan Harris"** Episode #224. *Making it RAIN with guest Tara Brach*

- Blog: **"The Inspired Dr. Mom"** *Meditation meets Military Jargon: RAIN vs OODA Loop.* Leslie Koenig, MD. https://lesliekoenig.wordpress.com/2020/02/22/meditation-meets-military-jargon-rain-vs-ooda-loop/

- YouTube/Podcast: **"The Jocko Podcast"** Podcast #120 time 1:20:10. https://www.youtube.com/watch?v=WzPyau4taT0

## Notes

# TECHNIQUE: TAPPING
## workbook

STRESSRELIEFSURVIVALGUIDE.COM | © 2020 LESLIE KOENIG, MD

# TAPPING
## EMOTIONAL FREEDOM TECHNIQUE

## WHAT IS TAPPING?

I found this helpful for myself- a skeptic who is closed off emotionally. This technique uses acupressure and meridians while talking through the emotion. The tapping spots are said to send energy directly to the parts of the brain which hold stress or negativity.

Tap each spot on the body with two fingers, about <u>5-10 times each spot.</u> Remember to breathe. Say this out loud as you go:

- "Even though I'm feeling anxious, I am in a safe place."
    - **Move to the next tapping spot after each phrase.**
- "I'm anxious. I'm overwhelmed. I'm overwhelmed by......"
    - **Keep talking, out loud, moving to the next tapping spot**
- "I'm anxious and that's understandable."
- "I'm overwhelmed and I forgive myself/I accept myself/I am still a good human being/I am in a safe place."
- "It's possible I can let go of all of this negativity."
- "I'm ready to let this go. I'm ready to be free of this overwhelm."
- "I can be happy in this life. I can relax now."
- TAKE A DEEP BREATH IN AND OUT

Tapping spots (if right handed):
1. Side of your left hand (Karate chop point)
2. Top of the head
3. Inner, then Outer right eyebrow (5-10 times each spot)
4. Below the right eye
5. Below your nose above cupid's bow
6. Chin
7. Under left collarbone
8. Right side ribs (easiest to use side of a fist) **RETURN TO STEP 2**

x 2-3

- Back to top of head and repeat steps 2-8 <u>three times</u>, then deep breath. This is ONE ROUND. Fill out worksheet 1-3. Do at least 3 rounds.

# TAPPING DIAGRAMS
#### WHERE DO I TAP?

**KARATE CHOP**

**TOP OF HEAD**

Rounds 2&3 start here

**IN & OUTER EYEBROW**

**UNDER EYE**

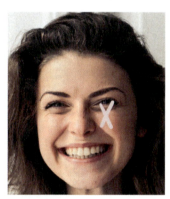

**UNDER NOSE**

**CHIN**

**UNDER COLLARBONE**

**RIBS**

**TAKE A BREATH**

go back to top of head x2

ONE ROUND COMPLETE

STRESSRELIEFSURVIVALGUIDE.COM | © 2020 LESLIE KOENIG, MD

# TAPPING NARRATIVE

## EMOTIONAL FREEDOM TECHNIQUE

**HELPFUL ADDITIONAL PHRASES:**

"I'm _____ right now. I'm so _____. I'm _____ because _____
I'm _____ but I also have times where I'm not so _____
I'm overwhelmed by _____ but I am safe. I'm starting to feel safe right now. I'm starting to feel like _____"
I am starting to see a way through this. I know that _____
and I release this _____ so I am free. I am free. I am _____

Keep going through the tapping until you get to a deep breath rest. This is **one round.** Copy this page and fill in as many times as you need for each question.

Go on to worksheet 1.

**AFRAID. ANGRY. ALONE. FRUSTRATED. PISSED OFF. EMBARRASSED. ANXIOUS. OUT OF CONTROL. SAD. DEPRESSED. ENRAGED. POWERLESS. HOPELESS. DESPERATE. IN PAIN. MIXED UP. CONFUSED. WRECKED. WORRIED. FAILURE. LOSER. WORTHLESS. NOTHING. PIECE OF S***. QUITTER. EMPTY. MISERABLE. BAD. HURT. CAN'T. TENSE. SICK. TIGHT. INADEQUATE.**

**Safe. Happy. Better. At peace. Calm. Fulfilled. Lighter. Strong. Loved. Capable. Joyous. Relaxed. Grateful. Thankful. Whole. Full. Warm. Hopeful. Healthy. Free. Liberated. Proud. Open. Beautiful. Empowered. Relieved. Optimistic. GOOD. Excellent. Worthy. Cared for. Victorious. Positive. Powerful Invincible. Awake. Clear. Enlightened. Alive. Present. Aware.**

# TAPPING WORKSHEET 1
### EMOTIONAL FREEDOM TECHNIQUE

**INSTRUCTIONS:** Track how you felt through this first practice round (karate chop x3 then deep breath). Go back and do another round then go to worksheet 2.

BEFORE

10
9
8
7
6
5
4
3
2
1
0

10
9
8
7
6
5
4
3
2
1
0

AFTER

What thoughts confused you?

Did any phrases feel very strong?

Did you gain any clarity?

# TAPPING WORKSHEET 2
## EMOTIONAL FREEDOM TECHNIQUE

**INSTRUCTIONS:** Track how you felt through this second practice round (karate chop x3 then deep breath). Go back and do another round then go to worksheet 3.

BEFORE

10
9
8
7
6
5
4
3
2
1
0

10
9
8
7
6
5
4
3
2
1
0

AFTER

**What thoughts confused you?**

**Did any phrases feel very strong?**

**Did you gain any clarity?**

STRESSRELIEFSURVIVALGUIDE.COM | © 2020 LESLIE KOENIG, MD

# TAPPING WORKSHEET 3

## EMOTIONAL FREEDOM TECHNIQUE

**INSTRUCTIONS:** Track how you felt through this third practice round

BEFORE

10
9
8
7
6
5
4
3
2
1
0

10
9
8
7
6
5
4
3
2
1
0

AFTER

What thoughts confused you?

Did any phrases feel very strong?

Did you gain any clarity?

# TAPPING WORKSHEET 4

**INSTRUCTIONS**: Write down 5 different questions or emotions in your life for which you think tapping will be helpful. **Schedule a time** in the next 4 weeks to tap on these. Now that you have the hang of it, feel free to use worksheet 5&6.

**QUESTION #1:** I STRUGGLE WITH_____(EMOTION)

SPECIFIC EXAMPLE:                  SCHEDULE DATE AND TIME TO TAP:

**QUESTION #2:** I WORRY ABOUT_____(EMOTION)

SPECIFIC EXAMPLE:                  SCHEDULE DATE AND TIME TO TAP:

**QUESTION #3:** I'M NOT HAPPY BECAUSE_____(EMOTION)

SPECIFIC EXAMPLE:                  SCHEDULE DATE AND TIME TO TAP:

*This is my biggest struggle*

**QUESTION #4:** I'M **NUMB.** I DON'T KNOW WHAT I'M FEELING._____

SPECIFIC EXAMPLE:                  SCHEDULE DATE AND TIME TO TAP:

**QUESTION #5:** I FEEL DISEMPOWERED WHEN _____(EMOTION)

SPECIFIC EXAMPLE:                  SCHEDULE DATE AND TIME TO TAP:

# TAPPING WORKSHEET 5

✓ **QUESTION #1:** _____

BEFORE I FELT...            AFTER I FELT...

MY THOUGHTS, INTUITIONS, REALIZATIONS...

✓ **QUESTION #2:** _____

BEFORE I FELT...            AFTER I FELT...

MY THOUGHTS, INTUITIONS, REALIZATIONS...

✓ **QUESTION #3:** _____

BEFORE I FELT...            AFTER I FELT...

MY THOUGHTS, INTUITIONS, REALIZATIONS...

# TAPPING WORKSHEET 6

✓ **QUESTION #4:** _____

BEFORE I FELT... AFTER I FELT...

MY THOUGHTS, INTUITIONS, REALIZATIONS...

✓ **QUESTION #5:** _____

BEFORE I FELT... AFTER I FELT...

MY THOUGHTS, INTUITIONS, REALIZATIONS...

**ADDITIONAL RESOURCES:**

**PHYSICIAN AND TAPPING COACH:**
- HTTPS://WWW.JILLWENER.COM/TAPPING

**ONLINE TAPPING COURSE:**
- HTTPS://THERESTTECHNIQUE.COM/COURSES/TAP-IN-HOW-TO-CREATE-YOUR-OWN-TAPPING-SEQUENCE

**YOUTUBE:**
- HTTPS://WWW.YOUTUBE.COM/WATCH?V=H7KY8YRECE0

# NOTES

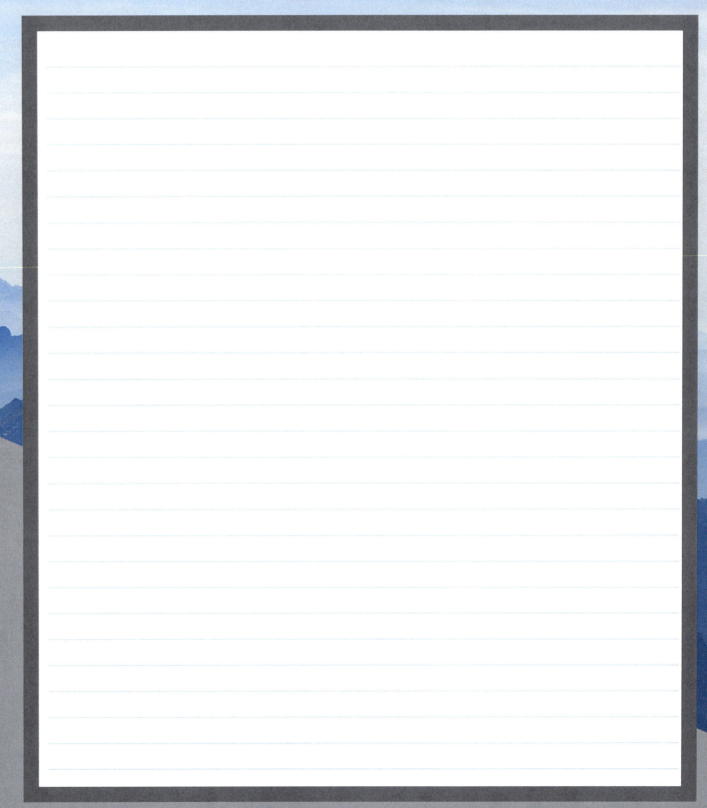

STRESSRELIEFSURVIVALGUIDE.COM | © 2020 LESLIE KOENIG, MD

# 333 OR 54321
*workbook*

STRESSRELIEFSURVIVALGUIDE.COM | © 2020 LESLIE KOENIG, MD

# 333/54321 SENSES

HIT THE RESET BUTTON

## OUT OF YOUR HEAD & INTO YOUR SENSES

When you're anxious, your thoughts can begin to spiral, or snowball into an avalanche of destruction. A story is building in your head and you can't get out. You are your own worst enemy, and you didn't even notice.Thankfully you now recognize these thoughts, but how to escape?

Sometimes it's overwhelming and other emotions layer in. Break the cycle with this easy technique:
- 54321 if you can remember them all, or
- 333 if you're so upset you forget which number meant what
.

STRESSRELIEFSURVIVALGUIDE.COM | © 2020 LESLIE KOENIG, MD

# 333 TECHNIQUE

> 3 things you *See*

> 3 things you *Hear*

> 3 things you *Feel*

Easy, right? In case of high emotion it can be hard to snap out of it. Get yourself away from the situation and do this technique. Once you go through it, move on to the 54321 technique.

STRESSRELIEFSURVIVALGUIDE.COM | © 2020 LESLIE KOENIG, MD

## 333 TECHNIQUE

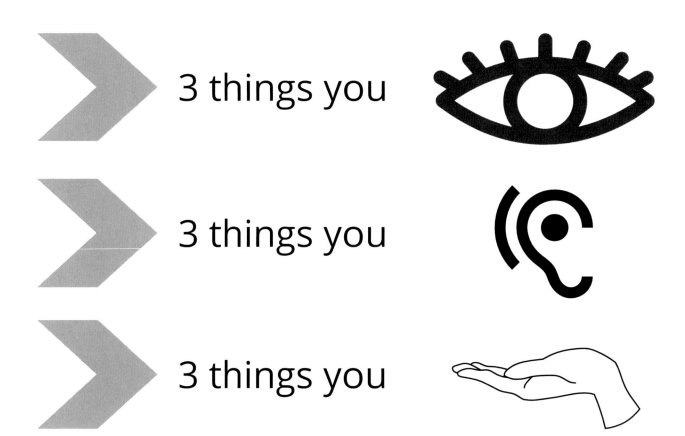

> 3 things you 👁

> 3 things you 👂

> 3 things you ✋

Visual icons for those who have trouble when in the throes of high emotion. When an emergency hits, sometimes the brain responds better to visuals than words!

# 54321 TECHNIQUE

> 5 things you *See*

> 4 things you *Hear*

> 3 things you *Feel*

> 2 things you *Smell*

> 1 thing you *Taste*

## 54321 TECHNIQUE

> 5 things you

> 4 things you

> 3 things you

> 2 things you

> 1 thing you

STRESSRELIEFSURVIVALGUIDE.COM | © 2020 LESLIE KOENIG, MD

# BONUS!

# 5-4-3-2-1 as a COUNTDOWN

## The 5 Second Rule

You have a moment of instinct that *Something* needs to change.  You have 5 seconds to **act** on it before your willpower and discipline evaporate.

Before you start, you have to commit to that when you hit 1, you will Act.  You don't have to know exactly how- just picture a rocket blasting off in another direction.  If you're in bed, you will physically do something different.  If you're pacing, you will physically do something different.  You will figure it out when you get to 1.  Just push yourself.

Count down with *intention*, with meaning.

5-4-3-2-1-**GO.**

*- Adapted from Mel Robbins "The 5 Second Rule."*

# 333/ 54321 WORKSHEET

GET IN TOUCH WITH YOUR SENSES

**INSTRUCTIONS**: As you now have clarity, you can choose which story to believe. You get to *make a choice*. You stopped the avalanche! So now, do you want to believe the negative version your mind created? Or create a new positive perspective that is healing and restorative? Create your new neural pathway to freedom.

| OLD STORY | NEW STORY |
|---|---|
|  |  |

# 333/ 54321 WORKSHEET

#### GET IN TOUCH WITH YOUR SENSES

**INSTRUCTIONS**: As you now have clarity, you can choose which story to believe. You get to *make a choice*. You stopped the avalanche! So now, do you want to believe the negative version your mind created? Or create a new positive perspective that is healing and restorative? Create your new neural pathway to freedom.

| OLD STORY | NEW STORY |
|---|---|
|   |   |

# BONUS! 54321 COUNTDOWN
## BLAST OFF TO SUCCESS

**INSTRUCTIONS**: Congratulations on taking action, even if it was just 5 feet in another direction. You tied a thought to a physical movement! You followed your instinct and laid a neural pathway for change. Write down what you *were* doing, then what resulted after blastoff.

### PRE BLASTOFF

I was laying in bed, knowing I would feel better if I got up to go workout but didn't feel like I could face the day

### POST BLASTOFF

After 54321 I committed to jumping up. Since I was up, I figured I'd put on my workout clothes. I walked 3 miles!

# NOTES

# BATTERY TECHNIQUE
*workbook*

STRESSRELIEFSURVIVALGUIDE.COM | © 2020 LESLIE KOENIG, MD

# BATTERY TECHNIQUE
## CHARGE UP YOUR LIFE

## YOU NEED A PEN

Wait, not a battery? Nope! Just a pen. This is a technique I invented myself and found great benefits. On the back of your left hand, draw a minus sign with a circle around it. On the back of your right hand, draw a plus sign with a circle around it.

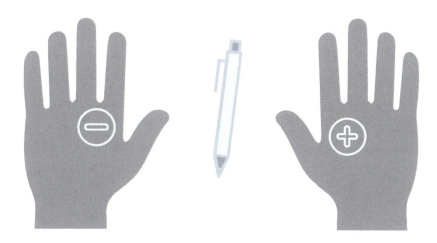

**You have just created the battery- it's you!**

Now set aside 5-10 minutes for this exercise. ***Try doing it around your house at first, going from room to room.*** As you progress, you can do it while sitting at your desk. Note your intrusive thought patterns.

When you are witnessing your thoughts being positive, put the pen in the right hand. When witnessing negative, move it to the other hand. Consider how you might change the thought so you can move it to the positive hand. While you're paying attention to your thoughts and making the note, hold the pen in both hands.

The goal is <u>not</u> to be positive or negative. When you hold the pen in both hands, you are *charging*. THIS is the goal! You are *noting your thoughts*. This is the technique!

STRESSRELIEFSURVIVALGUIDE.COM | © 2020 LESLIE KOENIG, MD

# BATTERY TECHNIQUE 1
## CHARGE UP YOUR LIFE

**INSTRUCTIONS**:
Step one: Notice your thought- is it positive or negative? While you witness, hold the pen between both hands.

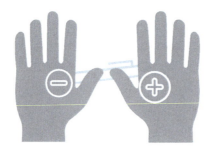 

**My thoughts are negative.**
 "I'm really
 anxious right now."

Step two: Put the pen in the left hand.

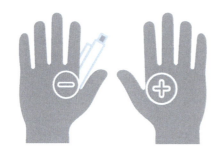 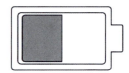

**OK how do I make my thoughts change to positive?**

Step three: Hold the pen in both hands

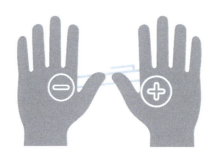 

STRESSRELIEFSURVIVALGUIDE.COM | © 2020 LESLIE KOENIG, MD

# BATTERY TECHNIQUE 2
#### CHARGE UP YOUR LIFE

I'm calm enough to do this technique. My hands aren't cramping. At least there's that.

Step four: Put the pen in the right hand.

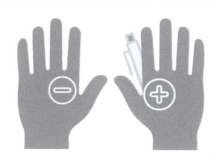

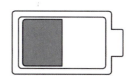

Nope. I'm losing it again... I think... I can't tell....

Step five: Hold the pen in both hands.

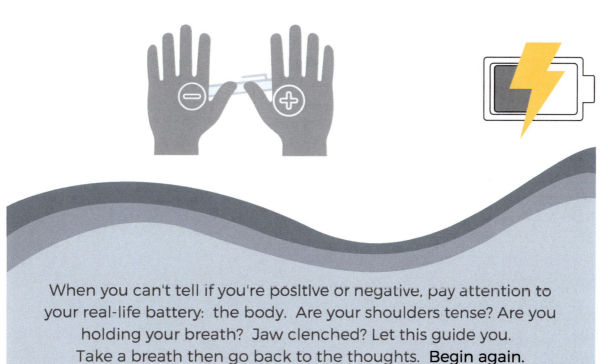

When you can't tell if you're positive or negative, pay attention to your real-life battery: the body. Are your shoulders tense? Are you holding your breath? Jaw clenched? Let this guide you. Take a breath then go back to the thoughts. **Begin again.**

STRESSRELIEFSURVIVALGUIDE.COM | © 2020 LESLIE KOENIG, MD

# BATTERY TECHNIQUE TRACKER

WRITE DOWN HOW MANY MINUTES YOU ACCOMPLISHED EACH DAY
GOAL: START WITH 5 MINUTES, END WITH 20 MINUTES

|  | WEEK 1 | WEEK 2 | WEEK 3 | WEEK 4 |
|---|---|---|---|---|
| MON | *5 minutes. Lots of distraction* | | | |
| TUES | | | | |
| WED | | | | |
| THURS | | | | |
| FRIDAY | | | | *20 minutes. I'm doing it randomly even without a pen!* |

STRESSRELIEFSURVIVALGUIDE.COM | © 2020 LESLIE KOENIG, MD

# BATTERY WORKSHEET

### CHARGE UP YOUR LIFE

**INSTRUCTIONS**: Write down your triggers from positive and back to negative. Did anything help recognize your thoughts so you you created a charge?

Negative:
My house is a mess

I looked at my hand and realized there was something Positive here

Positive:
I have a house to fill with messes

STRESSRELIEFSURVIVALGUIDE.COM | © 2020 LESLIE KOENIG, MD

# BATTERY WORKSHEET

CHARGE UP YOUR LIFE

**INSTRUCTIONS**: Write down your triggers from positive and back to negative. Did anything help recognize your thoughts so you you created a charge?

# NOTES

# MIRROR MEDITATION
## *workbook*

STRESSRELIEFSURVIVALGUIDE.COM | © 2020 LESLIE KOENIG, MD

# MIRROR MEDITATION
## WITH LOVING KINDNESS

### WITH LOVING KINDNESS

Sometimes you have to depend on yourself to bring yourself back from the brink. When no one is there to save you, you Must save yourself. Look in the mirror. Set aside 10 minutes.

Yes, 10 minutes. This is a long time (you'll see!) While a bathroom mirror is ok, I like a compact mirror better, to focus on just the eyes. There is plenty there to see and observe. For 5 minutes, silently clear your mind and observe. You may start to judge or want to look away- keep looking. Keep breathing. Keep observing.

After 5 minutes, begin the script as you continue to look in the mirror. **I promise you, these phrases are more powerful than they first appear.** If you begin to feel overwhelmed or start to cry, that's totally normal. It means you are doing it right and you are making a breakthrough! Research shows 20 minutes of the phrases for 8 weeks has been proven to shrink the areas of stress in the brain.*

*May you be happy.*

*May you be healthy.*

*May you be free from suffering.*

*May you live with ease.*

— *Sharon Salzberg*

May you be happy.

May you be healthy.

May you be free from suffering.

May you live with ease.

- Sharon Salzberg

May you be happy.

May you be healthy.

May you be free from suffering.

May you live with ease.

**C**ut out and tape to your bathroom mirror so you can review as you get ready.

Make a daily commitment to practices which are "onward leading," or are for the betterment of Who You Are. Cut out the bad habits, the negative mindset. Replace with small steps, like these phrases. This will lead you forward to where you want to go.

# MIRROR WORKSHEET 1

## WITH LOVING KINDNESS

**INSTRUCTIONS**: How did the meditation change once you introduced loving kindness? Did you look at yourself differently? Draw a picture of the person you wish to be, if you like. Your best self. Also fill out worksheet 5.

WHAT I SAW IN MYSELF

# MIRROR WORKSHEET 2

WITH LOVING KINDNESS

**INSTRUCTIONS**: Now, **with or without** a mirror, repeat the meditation for different areas or aspects of yourself. Write down a past self, a present self, and a future self to meditate on.

## Example:

When I was 4 and bullied on the playground

AREA A

The other day when I lost it at work/at someone

When I'm not able to walk anymore because I'm too old

AREA C

AREA B

# MIRROR WORKSHEET 2

### WITH LOVING KINDNESS

**INSTRUCTIONS**: Now, **with or without** a mirror, repeat the meditation for different areas or aspects of yourself. Write down a past self, a present self, and a future self to meditate on.

PAST

PRESENT                                         FUTURE

STRESSRELIEFSURVIVALGUIDE.COM | © 2020 LESLIE KOENIG, MD

# MIRROR WORKSHEET 3

## WITH LOVING KINDNESS

**INSTRUCTIONS**: Think of 4 different people and send the meditation phrases *towards them*

**Someone who has helped you**

**Someone you love**

**Someone you barely know**

**Someone you dislike**

# MIRROR WORKSHEET 4

### WITH LOVING KINDNESS

**INSTRUCTIONS**: Think of 4 different people and **imagine them sending the meditation phrases _towards you_**

Someone who has helped you

Someone you love

Someone you barely know

Someone you dislike

# MIRROR WORKSHEET 5

#### LOVING KINDNESS

RATE YOUR LEVEL OF HAPPY/SAD ON A SCALE OF 1-10

✓ **EXERCISE #1: MIRROR MEDITATION**

BEFORE I FELT...                                AFTER I FELT...

✓ **EXERCISE #2: MYSELF IN DIFFERENT AREAS/ERAS/ASPECTS**

BEFORE I FELT...                                AFTER I FELT...

✓ **EXERCISE #3: OTHER PEOPLE**

BEFORE I FELT...                                AFTER I FELT...

STRESSRELIEFSURVIVALGUIDE.COM | © 2020 LESLIE KOENIG, MD

# UGH, EW, NO

YEP IT SOUNDS OOEY GOOEY

## DON'T GIVE UP

What if some of these phrases you just can't stomach? The mirror meditation can use other phrases. Just start somewhere. Remember, *you're not getting graded* on this. There is *no judgement*. Pick one or come up with your own motivating phrase. Remember to dedicate 10-20 minutes for the phrase. This is enough time to overcome your past experience on the phrase and transform it into an effective tool.

I CAN DO THIS

GOOD. THIS IS GOOD.

GET SOME

I GOT THIS

I AM AT PEACE

SLOW IS FAST, FAST IS SLOW

WHATEVER IT TAKES

STRENGTH IN, WEAKNESS OUT

THIS TOO SHALL PASS

TRUST I SEEK, I FIND IN YOU

CALM, STEADY

_____

# LOVING KINDNESS
## AKA METTA MEDITATION

## THE SCIENCE

While I don't want to get too deep into the science here, it's fascinating how cutting edge technology is showing the literal effects on the brain of meditation- a thousands of years old practice.

It's not just self reported effects, but actual fMRI pictures showing the brain *changing*. This is also known as *neuroplasticity*.

> "Effects of mindful-attention and compassion meditation training on amygdala response to emotional stimuli in an ordinary, non-meditative state" Front Hum Neurosci. 2012; 6: 292.

The research article mentioned can be found here: https://www.ncbi.nlm.nih.gov/pmc/articles/PMC3485650/

There are countless more articles to dive into, should you be interested. Here are a few more references if you want to explore the benefits of meditation and loving kindness:

- https://www.**richardjdavidson**.com/
    - Researcher, author, one of "The 100 Most Influential People in the World" in 2006.
- https://www.**sharonsalzberg**.com/
    - Meditator, teacher, author
- https://**samharris**.org/
    - Neuroscientist, podcaster, author
- https://**davidvago**.bwh.harvard.edu/
    - Neuroscientist, meditator
- https://www.mindfulnesscds.com/
    - **Jon Kabat-Zinn**, founder of Mindfulness Based Stress Reduction (MBSR).

# NOTES

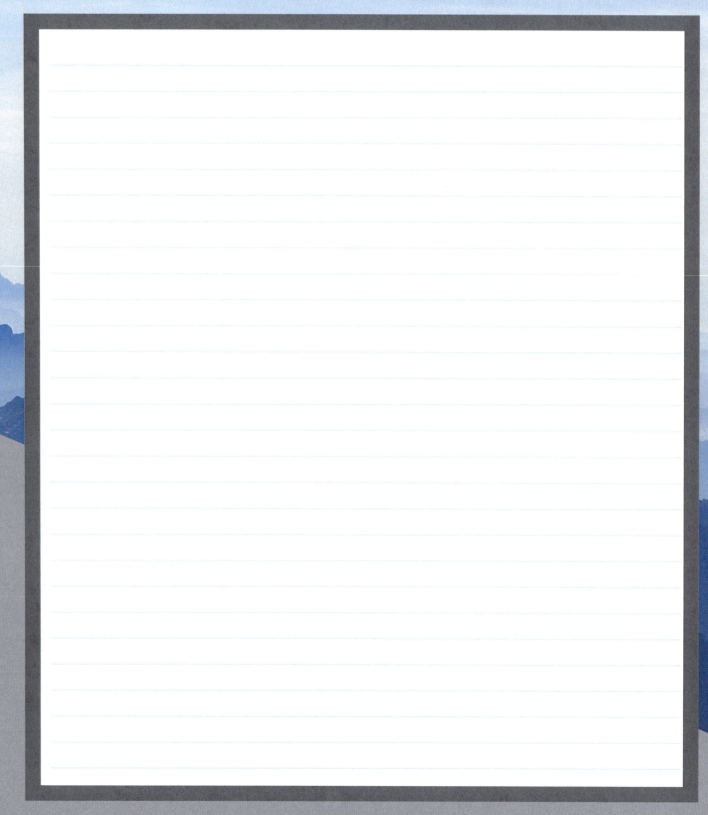

# HOT SHOWER
# ICE MAN
*workbook*

STRESSRELIEFSURVIVALGUIDE.COM | © 2020 LESLIE KOENIG, MD

# HOT SHOWER VS ICE MAN
## YOU ARE IN CONTROL

WHY BOTH?

**Hot showers are easy.** They are relaxing, require no talent or practice. They quickly calm people down. Water therapy has been known for centuries to induce sleepiness and a sense of peace.

For added bonus, try a shower fizzy for fantastic aromatherapy. *Don't know where to get one? How to make one?* In one of the worksheets below is a recipe. If you prefer baths, the shower fizzy is the same basic recipe for a bath bomb!

I would recommend you limit the shower to about 15 minutes, or about 5 minutes longer than once you would rate your anxiety at a 3. This allows you to have all the benefits without stripping the natural oils from your skin and causing a drying effect.

.

**Cold showers are something else entirely.** Start with hot then turn the tap cold. At first, the thought causes some mild anxiety, more from the anticipation of discomfort. No matter how calm or anxious you are, the first time is a shocker- **so jump right in!**

I came to the cold shower concept from Kundalini Yoga, then more intensely with the Wim Hof method. Did your mother ever throw you in a cold shower when having a tantrum? Mine did (I was 6 and wearing all my clothes). Instant tantrum stopper. Strangely, instant anxiety stopper as an adult too.

# HOT SHOWER FIZZY RECIPE

### AROMATHERAPY

**TOOLS:** Mixing bowl
Measuring cups
Molds (a muffin pan works great)

**INGREDIENTS:**

> 1 cup citric acid
> 2 cups baking soda
> 2 tbsp coconut oil or sweet almond oil
> ¼- ½ oz essential oil (lavender is great!)
> Spray bottle of Witch Hazel
> (Optional: 1 tbsp Polysorbate 80)

**INSTRUCTIONS:**

## Shower Fizzy

1. Sift Citric Acid and Baking soda together
2. Mix in oils
3. Use hands to mix
4. Add witch hazel until holds shape when squeezed with your fist
5. Part out into muffin tin
6. Pack down
6. Let sit 12-24 hours
7. Use by placing near water drain when needed.

---
Tip: Store in a display style apothecary jar or large glass container
---

## Bath Bombs

1. Sift Citric Acid and Baking soda together
   - If you want to add "fun" ingredients like Kaolin clay, Himalayan sea salt, colorants, etc. mix in here
2. Mix in oils
   - Optional: Can add Polysorbate 80 to help disperse oils in bath water
3. Use hands to mix
4. Add witch hazel until holds shape when squeezed with your fist
5. Part out into muffin tin
6. Pack down
   - Optional: Add decoration like dried flowers or eco friendly glitter to top
7. Let sit 12-24 hours

# HOT SHOWER WORKSHEET 1

### YOU ARE IN CONTROL

**INSTRUCTIONS:** In the white space, write 2-3 words to describe the emotion you felt when you entered the shower. In the gray space, write 2-3 words that helped the calming process.

**SHOWER 1:**

Essential oil used:

**SHOWER 2:**

Essential oil used:

**SHOWER 3:**

Essential oil used:

**SHOWER 4:**

Essential oil used:

STRESSRELIEFSURVIVALGUIDE.COM | © 2020 LESLIE KOENIG, MD

# ICE MAN WORKSHEET 1

## YOU ARE IN CONTROL

**INSTRUCTIONS:** Best done to jump start your day! Can also be used when you need to alter your focus from negative thoughts to awaken your senses. Done daily, this invigorating challenge will give you the confidence to face Anything.

**Kundalini yoga and Ayurvedic Medicine** recommends starting first with an almond, coconut, or sesame oil massage before getting into the shower. In ayurveda, the oil depends on your dosha type which can be tested with an online quiz or diagnosed by an ayurvedic practitioner.

- Jump right in to the coldest temperature shower you can stand.
- Keep your breathing even, maybe slowly saying "oh my heavens... oh my heavens...." or whatever holy phrase you wish to use!
- Be sure to get the arm pits (nerve center!) while massaging your arms, face, and chest
- Try getting in and out of the water a few times until it doesn't feel as cold anymore.
- Aim for 15 seconds the first time and build up to 3-5 minutes.
- Exceptions: For women, don't do during your period. Do not do after 7th month of pregnancy.

**Wim Hof, aka the Ice Man**, has developed a method to progressively take colder and colder showers with the aim of not only reducing stress, but also controlling the mind while improving the immune system. His system combines the cold therapy with very special breathing techniques if you wish to pursue further.

These breathing techniques are actually very helpful for **supporters** of an anxious person to understand **what the body goes through** when experiencing panic- however this is consciously induced, and so is controlled. *(see Guided Wim Hof Method Breathing.)*

- Start with a warm shower and turn cold.
- Dance! Sing! You are in control! You are the boss!
- Regulate your breathing, full breaths with full exhalations.
- Massage the skin and head.
- For 1 week do 15 seconds cold water at the end.
- Add 15 seconds every week until you build up and up.

# ICE MAN WORKSHEET 2

YOU ARE IN CONTROL

**INSTRUCTIONS:** Challenge yourself to a 20-day cold shower goal. Be sure to complete in 30 days. Check off each snowflake as you complete.

**Start Date:** _____   **End Date:** _____

| ☐ 15 SECONDS | ☐ 15 SECONDS | ☐ 15 SECONDS | ☐ 15 SECONDS | ☐ 15 SECONDS |
| --- | --- | --- | --- | --- |
| ☐ 30 SECONDS | ☐ 30 SECONDS | ☐ 30 SECONDS | ☐ 30 SECONDS | ☐ 30 SECONDS |
| ☐ 45 SECONDS | ☐ 45 SECONDS | ☐ 45 SECONDS | ☐ 45 SECONDS | ☐ 45 SECONDS |
| ☐ 1 MINUTE | ☐ 1 MINUTE | ☐ 1 MINUTE | ☐ 1 MINUTE | ☐ 1 MINUTE |

STRESSRELIEFSURVIVALGUIDE.COM | © 2020 LESLIE KOENIG, MD

# HOT SHOWER/ICE MAN SUGGESTED RESOURCES

Do It Yourself Bath/Shower Instructions and Supplies:

- BrambleBerry
- SoapQueen
  - http://www.soapqueen.com/
- DoTerra Essential Oils
- Young Living Essential Oils

Buy ready-made online or in store:
- http://lush.com/
- https://www.etsy.com/

Kundalini Yoga:
- https://www.3ho.org/

Ayurvedic Medicine:
- https://www.drnancylonsdorf.com

Wim Hof:
- Guided Breathing method
  - https://www.youtube.com/watch?v=tybOi4hjZFQ
- https://www.wimhofmethod.com/

# NOTES

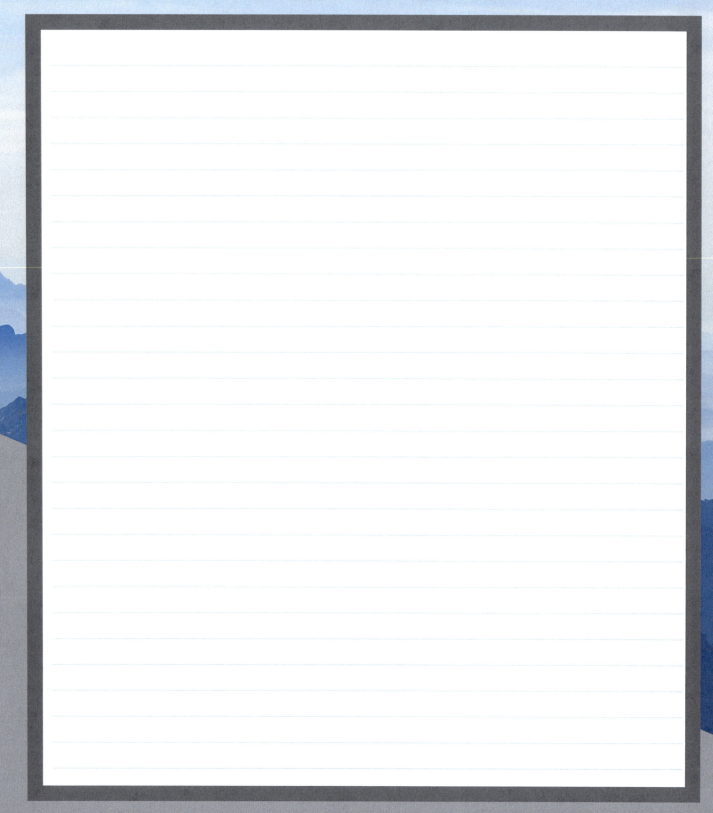

# THUMB SQUEEZE
*workbook*

STRESSRELIEFSURVIVALGUIDE.COM | © 2020 LESLIE KOENIG, MD

# THUMB SQUEEZE
## FINE MOTOR EXERCISE

## YOU HAVE ALL THE TOOLS

**Who has two thumbs and breathes?** You! This technique is a simple way to focus your breathing into your hands. You can do it eyes open or closed.

1. Make two loose fists, with the thumb inside
2. Breathing **in**, slowly **flex** your Right thumb
3. As you breathe **out**, slowly **relax** you Right thumb.
4. Try to time breath and movement so they start and stop together.
5. Do this for 5 rounds.
6. Relax, take a few breaths, open fist and relax.
7. Switch to left side.
8. Breathing **in**, slowly **flex** your Left thumb
9. As you breathe **out,** slowly **relax** you Left thumb.
10. Try to time breath and movement so they start and stop together.
11. Do this for 5 rounds.
12. Relax, take a few breaths with no thumb movement

Goals:
- Make the movements finer and finer until you are barely moving
- The breathing should be slow and deep

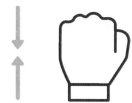 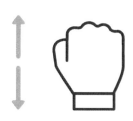

*- as taught by Oren Jay Sofer*

# THUMB SQUEEZE 1
### FINE MOTOR EXERCISE

**INSTRUCTIONS**: Breathe in as you squeeze your fist. Breathe out as you relax. Make the movement finer, more gentle, more light, until you are almost imagining it.

**RIGHT THUMB**

- BREATHE IN — SQUEEZE
- BREATHE OUT — RELAX

**LEFT THUMB**

- BREATHE IN — SQUEEZE
- BREATHE OUT — RELAX

STRESSRELIEFSURVIVALGUIDE.COM | © 2020 LESLIE KOENIG, MD

# THUMB SQUEEZE

FINE MOTOR EXERCISE

List 3 locations where you might use this technique- falling asleep, at work, etc.

If you have chronic pain, did you notice any reduction in your pain level?

Think about the cycle of in/out, squeeze/relax. What other fine motor exercises might work for you? Your toes, your shoulders?

Attention to something as simple as your thumbs creates an intense focus. Synaptic impulses are triggered in the central nervous system and rapid fire transmissions fan out peripherally. Action happens, which creates sensation, which goes right back up the chain.

From right brain to spinal cord to brachial plexus to motor functions and sensory nerves of the left thumb. It is a constant flow, back and forth. Acting, perceiving.

Imagine this chain of signals in your mind the next time you use your hands, your thumbs, and any part of the body. Create an awareness of how the brain connects to every single nerve ending you have. Your body Is a living machine.

# NOTES

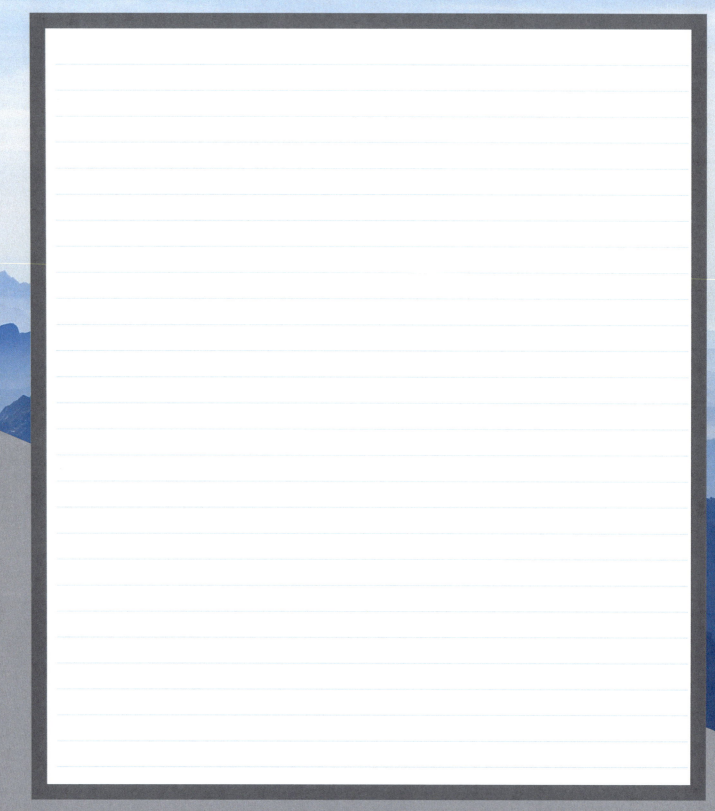

# IN THE HERE
# IN THE NOW

*workbook*

STRESSRELIEFSURVIVALGUIDE.COM | © 2020 LESLIE KOENIG, MD

# IN THE HERE
## WITH ARM EXERCISE

### DEVELOP PRESENCE

Stress is typically rooted in the thought of the past or the future. Once your mind is **truly present** in the moment, there is rarely anything to be truly stressed by. If you look around- unless you are being chased by a bear or teetering on the edge of a cliff, you're probably in a pretty safe place.

To remind ourselves of this, and to appreciate where we truly Are, use these phrases as you breathe in and out:

Breathe In → *In the here*
*In the here*

Breathe Out → *In the now*
*In the now*

*- Thich Nhat Hanh*

Just thinking this however isn't easy. Try a couple rounds and you'll notice your brain drift off into stress mode. Add this to keep you grounded, a technique I found to stay on track:

Wrap one or both arms in front of you, crossed. Move your fingertips from your elbows up to your shoulders as you think or speak the words "In the here, In the here" and breathing in. As you breathe out, move fingers down and repeat "In the now, in the now."

# IN THE HERE WORKSHEET 1
## DEVELOP PRESENCE

**INSTRUCTIONS**: This can be done even if your hands are tingling or cramping and gives you a felt-touch sense of your breathing.

Add an **ICE CUBE** to each hand & rub it on your arms if you need more presence

*In the here*
*In the here*

*In the now*
*In the now*

STRESSRELIEFSURVIVALGUIDE.COM | © 2020 LESLIE KOENIG, MD

# IN THE HERE WORKSHEET 2

### DEVELOP PRESENCE

✅ **EXERCISE #1: SPEAK OUT LOUD MEDITATION**

BEFORE I FELT...                      AFTER I FELT...

✅ **EXERCISE #2: SILENT MEDITATION**

BEFORE I FELT...                      AFTER I FELT...

✅ **EXERCISE #3: NO ARMS MEDITATION**

BEFORE I FELT...                      AFTER I FELT...

STRESSRELIEFSURVIVALGUIDE.COM | © 2020 LESLIE KOENIG, MD

# NOTES

STRESSRELIEFSURVIVALGUIDE.COM | © 2020 LESLIE KOENIG, MD

# PACED BREATHING
## *workbook*

STRESSRELIEFSURVIVALGUIDE.COM | © 2020 LESLIE KOENIG, MD

# PACED BREATHING
## IN HOLD OUT HOLD

## WHAT'S THE PACE?

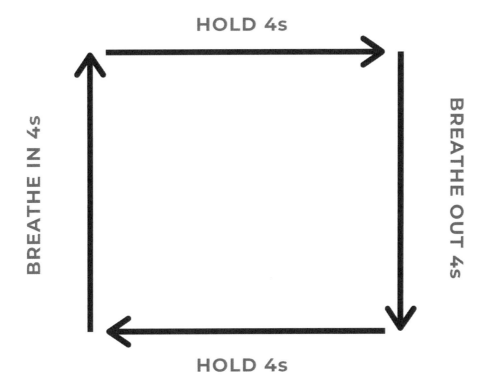

This technique I learned somewhere in my Navy training, probably during Officer Indoctrination School where we had to remain calm while treading water fully clothed while firehoses were aimed at us. You'll see it often attributed to Navy SEALS, probably for use in more extreme circumstances.

Whoever tries it and for whatever reason you need it, it works. Give it a 16 second try. Or more. Progress with a longer exhale, which lowers the heart rate (4,4,6,6).

# PACED BREATHING
## IN HOLD OUT HOLD

**INSTRUCTIONS**: IN 4 HOLD 4 OUT 4 HOLD 4

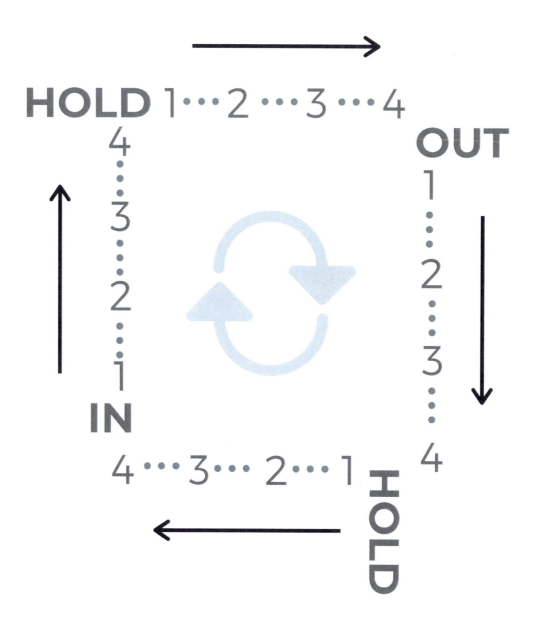

STRESSRELIEFSURVIVALGUIDE.COM | © 2020 LESLIE KOENIG, MD

# PACED BREATHING
IN HOLD OUT HOLD

**INSTRUCTIONS:** List all activities you do, big and small that you do regularly. Work, fun, etc. How many stars would you give it, if you were recommending to a friend? After you are done, question how to *limit your time* spending on one star activities. If you wouldn't return to a one star restaurant, why have one in your daily life?

STRESSRELIEFSURVIVALGUIDE.COM | © 2020 LESLIE KOENIG, MD

# PACED BREATHING
### IN HOLD OUT HOLD

**INSTRUCTIONS:** List all activities you do, big and small that you do regularly. Work, fun, etc. How many stars would you give it, if you were recommending to a friend? After you are done, question how to *limit your time* spending on one star activities. If you wouldn't return to a one star restaurant, why have one in your daily life?

STRESSRELIEFSURVIVALGUIDE.COM | © 2020 LESLIE KOENIG, MD

# PACED BREATHING

IN HOLD OUT HOLD

**INSTRUCTIONS:** List all activities you do, big and small that you do regularly. Work, fun, etc. How many stars would you give it, if you were recommending to a friend? After you are done, question how to *limit your time* spending on one star activities. If you wouldn't return to a one star restaurant, why have one in your daily life?

STRESSRELIEFSURVIVALGUIDE.COM | © 2020 LESLIE KOENIG, MD

# NOTES

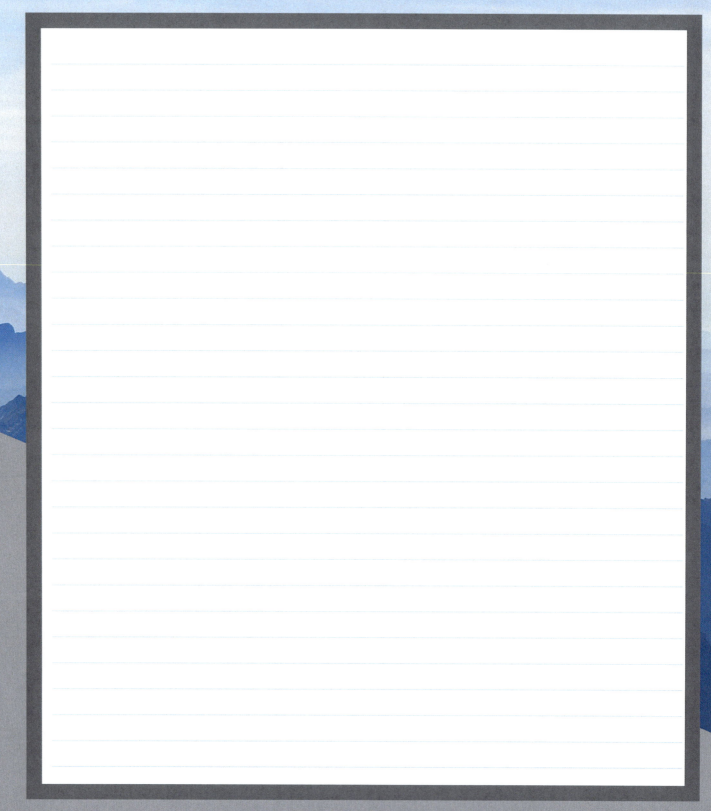

STRESSRELIEFSURVIVALGUIDE.COM | © 2020 LESLIE KOENIG, MD

# SHOCK THE SENSES
*workbook*

STRESSRELIEFSURVIVALGUIDE.COM | © 2020 LESLIE KOENIG, MD

# SHOCK THE SENSES
### REFOCUS

REFOCUS

In the escalation of stress and anxiety, there gets to be a point where the **rational brain just seems to short circuit.** At this point it's hard to even label it "fight or flight" in the mind. Every cell in your body starts to respond to the chemicals coursing through your veins, telling you something along the lines of DANGER BE SCARED YOU'RE GOING TO DIE RUN FIGHT I CAN'T BREATHE WHO AM I FIGHTING I CAN'T I CAN'T I CAN'T.....

You CAN stop this. You ARE able to regain control. Try something crazy. **Get outside your head**. Try stimulating two of the most sensitive of your 5 senses- taste and smell. The moment of "yeeek! Ew!" is a thought breaking the string of fear. This is your opportunity to take that alternative view and explore it further. Create an off ramp for the runaway semi truck your mind has become and pull it over, safely.

## BITE INTO A LEMON

## EAT/SMELL ESSENTIAL OIL

## EAT A TRAVEL SALT PACKET

# SHOCK THE SENSES

REFOCUS

**INSTRUCTIONS**: Three ideas are below, which can you apply to your situation? Can you think of other creative ideas to apply to your life?

*"I bring my lunch to work every day, I can easily bring a ziplock with a lemon slice in it"*

"Wow really sinking my teeth into the rind and all the sour juice coming out TOTALLY changed my focus."

"Actually I like smelling lavender or peppermint. It's nice to put it on the soft spot between thumb and pointer finger and inhale deeply."

*"I prefer a nice smell or a bitter taste. Certain essential oils are labeled "Dietary" or "Culinary" and are definitely shocking when you take a drop- like lime or lemon"*

*"I don't want to carry anything more than a salt packet I can get from any fast food place. It fits easily in my wallet."*

""Sour candy and strong mints always jolt me, maybe I can wrap one piece in plastic and fit it in my wallet. I also hate chewing my medicine but that could work."

# SHOCK THE SENSES WORKSHEET

YOU'RE OK NOW.  WRITE DOWN YOUR THOUGHTS.

# NOTES

# RE BREATHING
*workbook*

STRESSRELIEFSURVIVALGUIDE.COM | © 2020 LESLIE KOENIG, MD

# REBREATHING
## SLOW, CALM, EASY

## PAPER BAG

**Hyperventilation: What are some symptoms?**
- Numbness all over
- Tingling all over
- Chest wall tightness
- Chest pain
- Shortness of breath
- Hand cramping
- Feeling of "I'm going to die" or "impending doom"
- Nausea
- Disorientation
- Weakness
- Feeling faint
- Distorted vision

**Treatment:** REBREATHING and **go to the ER. Some of these are also symptoms of other medical problems. You cannot tell without a proper medical exam.**

# BREATHE IN & OUT INTO A PAPER BAG

STRESSRELIEFSURVIVALGUIDE.COM | © 2020 LESLIE KOENIG, MD

# REBREATHING

SLOW, CALM, EASY

## WHY A PAPER BAG?

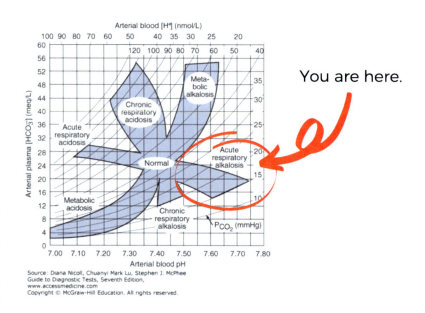

Panic mode will make you go into a high adrenaline state. This makes you breathe faster, as your body thinks you're preparing to run from a saber-toothed tiger versus attack it with a spear.

Normally oxygen is breathed in and your body processes it into carbon dioxide ($CO_2$). When you breathe too fast, you **drive out CO2** faster than your body makes it. In the body, carbon dioxide is normally dissolved in the blood so it balances your pH.

 ACID  BASE

Too little $CO_2$ and your pH goes up. or into the base state of alkalosis (the opposite of acidic). This causes a bunch of chemistry changes in the body which leads to the cascade of symptoms. You need to bring $CO_2$ back into the balance.

To bring back $CO_2$ to regain balance, you need to either
1. Slow down your breathing (you can actually hold your breath for up to and over 2 minutes- I've done it in a controlled setting!)
2. Store the $CO_2$ you breathed out and take it back in. Paper bag.

# REBREATHING WORKSHEET 1

SLOW. CALM. EASY.

### DEVELOP AN ACTION PLAN

You are now back from the ER and were told it was stress or anxiety. You may worry this is going to happen again. This is entirely normal, but a goal is now to decrease this anticipatory anxiety. Your doctor and a mental health care professional should now be involved to help you through this. Answer the questions and make a plan for when/if it occurs, then seek professional help if it happens again.

**What were some early symptoms that let you know you were about to have an attack? Heart racing? Sweating?**

**Where did/will you store your paper bag for when/if you need it?**

**Who will you call, where will you go in case of emergency?**

- 911
- Nearest emergency room
- Anxiety hotline
  1-800-64-PANIC (72642)
- My counselor/therapist

**Was there anything else that helped during your attack?**

# REBREATHING WORKSHEET 2

SLOW. CALM. EASY.

**INSTRUCTIONS**: Stress that induces a panic attack or anxiety attack can be very frightening. Even in the days after an attack, you may feel extremely drained and everything feels difficult. This is normal. Think of people who you can reach out to who can help. Any activities that usually help, like hiking or petting your dog/cat?

SUPPORT CIRCLE

# NOTES

# NOTHING CAN BRING YOU PEACE BUT YOURSELF.

RALPH WALDO EMERSON

Made in the USA
Monee, IL
16 October 2023

44552835R00062